A Collection of Poems by

Black British Poet

Remeaise Irish-Downes

To my dear mother,

the woman who inspired me

every day of my life.

Contents

Part Three
POEMS ABOUT ISSUES THAT CONCERN ME

Part Four
CARING THOUGHTS

Preface

First, let me say thank you for turning to the preface to learn more about the content of my poetry book. I originally began writing five years ago after passing my GCSE exam at the age of fifty-seven. I realised I had a love for creative writing and told my teacher I was going to write my autobiography, but due to the loss of my uncle's wife, I ended up caring for him. He was like a father to me. When my uncle passed, I had time to resume typing my book. I opened my laptop and couldn't remember what I had filed the work under.

I cried for a few days, feeling like someone had just pressed the delete button and erased my life. You may think I was a bit dramatic. I made a promise to myself to start and finish this book, as I have a problem sometimes with finishing projects—unless I have a deadline set for them.

I decided after a couple of days to just pull myself together and start typing again. I wrote a title and began typing and continued for two pages. I realised I was writing poetry, so I carried on until the piece was finished. I typed the poem in two hours. I had mixed emotions about what I had typed—this poem about my life—and I was buzzing and excited at the thought that maybe this was the way to write about my life.

My goal was to write every day but not be hard on myself if I didn't, as I also worked a couple days a week on shifts at my local airport. My goal was to complete my book in one year, which I achieved.

The poems I have written will take you on a journey of love, loss, relationships, motherhood, family, food, and well-being—and also things that concern me. I am confident my book will have something you can resonate with or had similar experiences enduring.

My reason for writing was initially to document my life for my children, but I found it was a time of reflecting on my life, seeing how I had grown to become the person I am today, and following my dreams, inspiring people to never give up on their dreams and to have faith and to believe in themselves.

I never let age stop me from trying something new; after all, life is for living and I have the chance to do so. I am living my best life and so can you.

This is the start of my writing journey. My poetry book is completed, and the autobiography has reached eighteen thousand words, so there is more to come.

I truly believe I was given the blessings of a kick-start to my writing journey, and I do love God's plan. The poetry writing has led me to attending poetry events and on occasion signing up for open mike; it has also given me an excuse to travel to Amsterdam with my daughter for a poetry event, at which I read one of my poems. I was shown a lot of support and enjoyed the experience.

And now, I hope you enjoy the experience of reading my poetry.

Part One

POEMS ABOUT FOOD, WELL-BEING, AND MOTHERHOOD

Sauce

She is confident in her radiance
and comes in many colours.
She can be poured, spread, or even squirted,
and when she coats your surface,
she will cling and wrap herself around you.
She is a force to be reckoned with.

She may burn you, but she won't kill you;
for she is only seasoning you
to enhance the flavours she brings out in you.
She can be medicinal and make you sweat,
you wouldn't even know it, till your shirt's wet.
So next time you see her, prepare your senses.

Spice

Do you want to learn how to cook?
You might need a cookery book.
People from the Caribbean didn't need a recipe;
it's part of their legacy.
Your grandmother, she never read one yet,
for she was taught by the best.

She was a practical learner.
It was her job before going to school
to collect all the spices your grandfather needed
for him to marinate the meats.

His business was cooking for the local government.
It was her job to use the pestle and mortar
to pound all the spices together.

The spices were sprinkled into the mortar,
measuring with only the eyes.
The meats would be rubbed in with seasoning
and left for an hour to marinate.

This was a skill learned over time,
continuing the same routine.
Her siblings learned these skills too.
Everyone had to chip in and get the preparations done.
It was for the various meals of the day. The proof was
in the eating, all the authentic spices that laced the
meats—so succulent in your mouth.

Solitude

The time I spent in complete silence.
The space that I desperately needed
to replenish my mind.
Immerse in being just me
and reconnecting to my inner child,
giving her the energy she desires.

Space to explore in complete silence, without distractions.
Omitting the negative people from my life
who choke my creativity and growth.
I'll live each day like it's my last, for tomorrow is not a promise.
So don't waste time doing unnecessary things;
immerse me in just being me, myself, and I —
not mum, wife, or carer to others—some selfless time.
Treasure and replenish my mind for my own well-being.
I deserve that as a human being.
I understand that I am worth it—self-love, positive thinking,
and doing it solo.
Develop my new goals in spoken word and writing my autobiography.
And a few other things to add to the list:
explore new places, new inspirations around the globe.
These things make up solitude for me.
The solitude we all need sometimes, just to reflect on who we are,
what we have achieved in life, and what is left to work on.

Natural

Natural beauty, nothing fake about me,
amazingly creative with what God gave me.
Thanks to the beauty that lies within,
unconditionally loving the blessings of my body.
Reaching for the stars that are making me shine.
I appreciate that this is my time.
Love to the Almighty, for he is divine.

I spread my roots to anchor me down,
to make me stable beneath the ground.
You sprinkle your blessing, so pure from the sky,
to feed me the nutrients I so desire.
When I am ready, I will rise above the soil and bare my all.

Evolve

I've been on this planet since 1958,
so I have been evolving since a baby.
Getting from crawling to standing,
taking my steps at seven months.

My next milestone was speech,
expressing my daily needs.
Starting school helped me
to evolve into a junior,
making conscious choices,
really thinking for myself.

I was able to develop creativity
that was waiting to burst right out.
Learning all the knowledge,
directed in the path for success.

Slowly evolving in a career path,
which evolved dramatically.
Taking a chance to explore other skills
constantly throughout my life.

Craft

Women came together to use their craft
to construct a blanket for my child.
They used my clothes that I wore as an infant,
which showed my growth over the years.
The realization of the history in the materials
that were used for making the items that wrapped my body,
that kept me warm on a daily basis.
I've acknowledged all the women
who have touched the clothing.

They sorted them into colour piles,
carefully cutting them into squares
to creatively sew them together again.
For all the women in my family
who have come together to recycle my clothing,
to make this new patchwork, then turn it into something else
that will tell my history, to be passed on to my children.
I thank you for loving me and for acknowledging my life,
for making the coverings, for protection and healing.

A Recipe from a Happy Mother

A recipe from a happy mother.
Just a little reminder from me.
These are the ingredients I have used to help raise you
into the fine young adults you have grown into today.

Ingredients:
100% love and care
100% food and clothing
100% education 24/7
50% nurse
25% social worker
50% doctor
25% wife
50% painter and decorator
25% cleaner
50% cook

My priorities change according to age and stages of your growth,
and also my growth.
You are at an age when you should be planning your own recipe.
I am not going to be around forever,
but as I always say: My recipe
is forever changing for the betterment of us all.

Ink

As I descend into your well and lubricate my nib
that will help me to make my mark,
today, I thank you.
There are many ways I can make my mark
to express my words for all to see,
but I decided to choose you.
You are natural and come from the sap
taken out of the pine tree.
Like ink, you've been around as far back
as 2500 BC.
My words are simply a way to express
how grateful I am to have you in my life.
You give me the energy charge that I need,
right now, so I can speak about you on this day.
You have made an impact on many people's lives.

I sincerely thank you.

Static

Static in a job that I've worked in for so long,
trying to think of why I've been playing the same old song.
Angry at my life for panning out this way,
thinking of ways to enjoy my days.

Intellectuals need to use their brains,
comparing my life to the people on the train.
The train has made a sudden stop;
we're completely in the dark,
static in the tunnel—will we ever disembark?
I need to make some changes;
life is too short.

When I arrive home, I will find my passport,
will book us a flight—I don't care where to.
Just me and you, we can be static,
in a new place with a view.

Laughter

Laugh your loudest laugh;
this is what makes you young.
After laughing, there is a type of calm;
reflect on what was funny,
grow this skill each day.
It'll keep the wrinkles away.

Life is way too short, so just get on and live.
Unapologetically, do what makes you happy.
Happiness is your responsibility.
Remember, it's your life.
You don't want any regrets.
Put your laughter to the test.
Just like sending a letter to someone.
Please remember the happy times.

Grandma

Oh, I wish I knew my grandma,
but it was never meant to be.
She was a million miles abroad from me.
I remember writing her a letter
when I was about seven years old;
I also remember her reply.

Oh, I wish I'd met my grandma;
what a lovely time we would've had.
I would inherit her recipes
and hide them from my dad.

Oh, I wish I could hug my grandma
and tell her all my woes.
Unfortunately, that will never happen;
she sadly passed away.

So every grandma I meet—
well, the ones who live on my street—
I try to visit them
and have a cup of tea.
We build a lovely friendship;
they love me for being just me.
I do some things to help them,
as if they're my family.

I love my entire grandmas
for what they can bring to the table.
Their wisdom, knowledge, and understanding
kept me skilled in sewing and knitting throughout my life.
If you haven't got a grandma,
there are plenty out there you can help.
Remember they have so much to give,
so don't forget to look after them.
They are precious little gems.

(Not of the salad kind.)

Legacy

I have been taught by the best generations past down.
Mother was blessed as she wore the crown.
She passed on all her skills to me:
dressmaking, hairdressing, and cookery.
Who needs to be rich when you're rich in legacy?

It provides me with food and clothes on my back.
An occasional good hairstyle to finish the look.
Self-sufficiency when you have little funds;
you can walk proud like the rest,
wearing your Sunday best.

All skills, never taken for granted,
and now they've been handed right down
to my young Nubian children.
You shall one day wear the crown.

Crush

I'm moving considerately in one direction,
trying to find a place to stand.
People are moving too closely, invading my personal space.
Now someone is so close to me that they are leaning on my back.
Bodies rushing in from all directions—I feel a panic attack.

I understand that we all have somewhere to go;
we must think about each other's personal space.
After all, you wouldn't like me standing right up
in front of your face.

Please consider the little people,
whilst leaning to reach on the bar.
Please be aware of your personal hygiene;
consider using deodorant.
Armpits above me whilst holding on
can be overpowering.

Next time you're on the train,
remember you're causing my nostrils pain.

Part Two

POEMS ABOUT RELATIONSHIPS, FAMILY, LOVE, AND LOSS

I Need Answers

Where were you?
You said that you loved me,
that I was your special girl.
You were not there.

Where were you?
When I was starting school,
I needed a uniform and support from you.
You were not there.

Where were you?
With my mother by my side,
the first day I was drawing you,
the man I felt was true.
Yet you were not there;
only my mother was true.

Where were you?
When I had my first Holy Communion,
this should have been a family union.
My mother, my godfather,
and godmother were there.
You were not there.

Where were you?
When I made the transition into high school,
I needed love and guidance from you.
You were not there.

Where were you?
When I needed your help
as I made my way through life.

You were not there.
Where were you?
When I started college and
needed books and equipment.
You were not there.
My mother was.

Where were you?
When I graduated and my mother sat proudly
beside an empty seat.
You were not there.

Where were you?
When I started my first job,
I came home proud with my first wage packet.
Oh! You were not there.

Where were you?
When I bought my first home
and had your first grandchild.
You were not there.
My mother was.

Where were you?
When I had your second grandchild.
You were not there.
My mother was there.

Where were you?
When I was getting married,
you were meant to walk me down the aisle
and stand proudly by my side.
Oh! It was too late.
Sadly, you were called by the Lord Almighty.
My mother was there, but only in spirit.

She stood proudly by my side.
Sadly, the good Lord had called her too.

Her reward for always being there,
for her only surviving child out of three,
was to finally rest in peace
in her homeland of Jamaica.

Still, she was with us
when my husband and I got married.
She blessed us both on our day
in front of her two grandchildren.

Role Model

She is small and elegant.
She is protective of her own.

She carries her little handbag
everywhere she goes.

Her shoes are always polished.
Her clothes are immaculate.

She's very independent
and won't take any lip.

She goes to work each morning;
she's always in a rush.

The neighbours say, "There goes Alma!
She's running for her bus".

She does her shopping on Fridays,
and Saturday mornings too.

She always has her routine,
and this is what it is:
Saturday for marinating the chicken,
then rinse her peas and place into the bowl to soak.

Sunday she stews down the chicken in her dutch pot,
then she cooks the rice and peas.

Sunday is also her day of rest and going to her church,
praising to the good Lord for knowing what she's worth.

Every night she says her prayers;
she asks God for these three things:
wisdom, knowledge, and understanding.
For he is her guide in everything; and she lived by good morals.
That was my mum.

The little handbag mentioned in the poem was actually me.
Rest in peace.

Mr. Right

Thirty-eight,
the clock was ticking.
Which lucky man
would I be picking?
I own my own house,
that was the plan.
Now I need
to find a nice man.

Well, I need to be considerate;
men these days, my age,
usually, have a child or two or three,
with different baby mummies.
What hope is there for me?

My goals are set high;
I wanted to find Mr. Right,
so I made a checklist:
no kids, a good job,
older than me preferably.

Now I need to check my list again,
then change Mr. Right to Mr. Suitable.
People make mistakes.
Relationships break down.

So the goals of finding a man,
well, it's looking kind of grim.
Where the hell am I going to find him?

I'm not getting younger.
Does the age really matter?

Well, it does to me.

So my previous goals,
I have to make exceptions.
He could have one child,
good job,
age, not a problem,
as long as he's mature.
Well, am I asking for too much?
I don't think so.

Living a Double Life

When I met you, you were not the one.
You were just the messenger.
A friendship built over six months,
you decided to ask me out.
I thought you were a decent guy,
but you knew you were living a lie.

Time went by, and a commitment was promised
with a ring—you were doing the right thing.
You asked my mother for the blessing.
She said she'd wait and see
before she'd introduce you to the family.

She didn't give her blessing:
"An engagement ring is not a marriage.
Things could change quite quickly".
My mother was psychic, you know.
She had already sussed how this would go.

Eight months in a relationship,
things were hunky-dory.
Then you dropped the bombshell news:
You were going to be a daddy.
You protested you didn't know.

You told me that you bumped into your ex
and noticed she'd put on a lot of weight.
It was the signs of motherhood so near;
she confessed it was your child.

I told you to go back and raise your family.
It was the early days for you and me.

I would rather a child be raised by her mother and father.
The look of innocence on your face, as if you didn't know,
then I try to be mature about the situation.
I heard the words "I love you, you're the one
I want to build my life with".
I swallowed the idea that you really cared for me.

Start acting like a dad, I said,
you never know if it's the only child you'll have.
Well, things carried on from there.
You tried to live the life of being a dad.
You lost your job and then went crazy,
smoking and drinking heavily.

I tried to give you moral support.
After all, I was your girlfriend and stood by your side.
It wasn't easy, as you always worked hard and
clung to your pride.

You were asked to DJ at a little club.
I heard an announcement on the radio
the night before the gig.
I decided to go and show support,
and asked your sister to go with me.

As we arrived at the club, it was just getting started.
We descended down the stairs. You were there.
By the facial expressions on the other DJs' faces
and the finger-slapping action,
I knew you were caught out on something.
You didn't look up to acknowledge me; we're supposed to be engaged.
This is the way you were treating me, as if I was a nobody.
I entered the room without paying, you came out shouting yow!
I turned and asked you, "Are you speaking to me"?
You replied, "I would like to speak to you".

I replied, "This is not the way you greet me".
And we're supposed to be engaged.
I noticed a group of girls who had just walked in.
I recognised your ex-girlfriend
from a photo album previously showed.
Your friend came over and asked me for a dance.
I accepted to be polite.

I held my head high; I knew what was going on.
It seemed you never thought I would come to the event.
You came over again and tried to speak,
reminding me we're engaged.

Your sister thought it was time to leave,
as you were acting quite strange.
We ascend the stairs to get in her car;
you called your brother to follow us.
Your sister was scared.

Her foot was down on the pedal;
we managed to escape out of sight.
We arrived at the other venue
for an evening of music and fun.

Your sister was asking what just went on.
I explained you were caught in a lie.
And you were in the wrong.

We went to another event to make a night of it.
The DJ was playing, "Young, Free and Single",
and later on, the song "Casanova" also played.
These songs are a reminder of that night's experience
and depicted the events for me that night.

Now the truth has unfolded:
something was definitely going on.

Early the next morning, I visited your home;
all would be revealed.
I had a chat with your whole family.
They knew nothing of our engagement,
of the plans for a big party,
which, after the response from my mother,
there wasn't ever going to be one.

Your parents were very fond of me,
and we were hit with this shocking news.
They told you, "You need to do the right thing".
They believed I was the right girl for you.
You now had the responsibility for your child;
you had to stop running around so wild.

Valentine's Day arrived—we were meant to be together—
but when I arrived at your home, we had a little guest.

I encouraged you to be there for your child,
but I didn't need her rubbed in my face.
She kept on crying, and I could not stand the noise;
it spoilt it all for me, and this was more than I could bear.
This relationship was not going to work; I wished I wasn't there.

Watching you play happy families,
I decided this wasn't going to be my life.

The lies and deceit, I found out from friends
who didn't live on the same street.
In fact, thirty miles away, how bizarre is that?
Two sets of friends, who did not know each other.
The stories all added up, that my boyfriend had never left his ex.

The stories I was told by him were a lie.
I needed to catch him out and prove to him I'm no fool.
Well, the door opened and in he came,
as he did not sleep at home that night.
I asked him whose bed he slept in.
He was too quick to reply.
He stayed with his mate till late.

Well, I said, we are not going to be engaged anymore,
for telling me all the lies.
He was quick to say you girls like to listen to gossip.
Amazing, how the gossip was true.

You were seen in the early hours of the morning
coming out of your ex's house.

What Goes around Comes Around

Isn't it funny how men have short memories?
They forget things so easily.
Going around with their freedom,
preying on innocent young women,
hurting them in so many ways.
Well, remember, you need to stop
and think about how to treat a woman.

What goes around comes around.
They experience fatherhood,
the problems that come with it.
They are blessed with a daughter
and expect other men to respect their little girls.

Wait a minute...you want another man to respect your girl child?
Did you respect other people's daughters
when you dated them back in the day?
You went around sowing your seeds all over the place.
What you sow is what you reap.
Now it's hit you below the belt;
you're trying to dictate to your teenage child
what she can and can't do,
or with whom she can or can't go on a date.

Oh! The teenage years were such a tricky time.
Now you know how it feels to be a father
when your daughter comes home
pregnant from a man your age.
You, as a man, needed to set the example,
so please practice what you preach.
It's no good coming to me with your speech.
I remember when you came complaining to me
about the problems of being a parent and

your daughter not coming home.
Sleeping out with older men; your memory was short.
You forgot about hurting all the women you went out with.

Well, now you feel the pain that many parents feel
when trying to protect their young girls
from getting hurt or not finding true love,
or getting pregnant at a young age.
I could go on and on, but life is too short.

Don't Complain to Me

It took me awhile to see,
thought you were the one for me.
So much jealousy.
Don't complain to me.

So she left you.
Men don't get it.
You find a good woman,
but the grass is always greener
on the other side.
Don't come crying to me.

She had the sense to identify
you were one big lie;
you want my sympathy.
I told you, what you sow is what you reap.
Don't come crying to me.

I've moved on now, getting on with my life.
You said you were going to make me your wife.
A promise is a comfort to a fool.
You thought you were being so cool.
Don't come crying to me.

You have the nerve to think
I would feel sorry for you.
How low are you able to sink?
She finally found out you're a dirty flirt,
wearing your designer shirts.
Don't complain to me.

So you decided
who you wanted to settle down with.
It's too late to heal my pain.
I definitely won't be fooled like that again.
Please don't come complaining to me.

Travelling Solo

For years, New York has been calling me.
I was the last to visit my family.
(I'm travelling solo.)

I decided to take a trip.
Damn, life is running out too quickly.
(I'm travelling solo.)

When I arrived at the airport,
the security asked for my passport.
The plane ride was turbulent,
just like my emotions.

My first time travelling,
my hair began unravelling.
I pulled myself together.
I began to write some plans.
(I'm travelling solo.)

There's someone I've been thinking about,
someone I really need to find.
It's been rushing in and out of my mind.

The plane landed safely.
I picked up all my things.
(I'm travelling solo.)

Whilst heading for the exit,
I had a major thought:
Is he dead, or is he alive?
Will I ever find him?

The taxi came, then drove me to the hotel.
No one at the reception desk,
so I had to ring the bell.
(I'm standing here solo.)

"Welcome to the Big Apple",
the man said to me.
"Here you are, madam, this is your key".
I took the elevator, ascended to my room.
I really tried to settle in.
I was tired from the journey.
(I travelled here solo.)

Well, I lay on the bed to rest my weary body.
A crazy thought just rushed through my head.
I phoned the operator and told her about my plan.
I was on a mission to find an old family man.
(I'm sitting there solo.)

She asked me for his name,
and I felt a little ashamed.
She might be able to find him,
much to my surprise!
There were three people listed
with the same initials and surname.
(I'm sitting there solo.)

She gave me the numbers to all three.
I thanked her for her help.
Shivering in my skin,
my thoughts were running wild,
the anxiety was too much.
(I'm sitting there solo.)

I plucked up the courage and decided to phone,
wondering if one of them would maybe be at home.
(I'm sitting there solo.)

I started with the first one.
It rang for quite a while.
I tried the second number.
There still was no reply.

I dialled the final number,
and I waited patiently,
hoping that he'd answer
and help me mentally.
(I'm sitting here solo.)

The phone was just ringing,
I was going to hang up.
I was feeling kind of low.
Just as I put the handset down,
I heard a voice say ,"Hello"?

I was in a state of panic,
I didn't plan what to say.
I had to think quickly.
I said, "Hi, I am trying to
contact Lloyd Irish".
The woman said to me, "Please,
could you ring back later?
My husband would know that name".
Who should I say called?
I said, "A friend of the family".
(I sat in shock solo.)

I pondered, should I phone back?
What the hell would I say?

Should I just come out with it?
(I'm sitting here solo.)
I braved this big moment
to find out what I could.
I waited patiently, then redialled later on.
The phone line was busy—I had to try again.

It rang three times, and then I heard a voice:
"Hello, what can I do for you"?
(I'm sitting there solo.)

"Good evening, sir! I am trying to locate Lloyd Irish".
He replied to me, "I've known his sister for many years".
I'm now in complete shock.
Here I have the link.
(I'm sitting there solo.)

I confessed: "I am Lloyd's daughter".
He explains to me, "Please forgive him.
He lives in another state.
I will make some phone calls
to try to track him down.
It has been so lovely to speak to you,
I hope you'll stick around".
(I'm sitting there solo.)

Two hours passed, then I received a call.
It was the man I spoke to earlier.
"I've found your dad's location.
It's in Cleveland, Ohio state.
Now, please remember what I said
and let him clear the slate".
(I'm sitting there solo.)
I told him, "I have things to say.
I had to clear my chest.

For all the years he disappeared,
my mother did her best".
So the number that he gave me,
I thanked him so much.
I hoped it was my father
who would be answering the phone.

But, when I made the call, the woman who answered
the phone said, "Sorry, he's not at home right now.
Who should I say called"? I quickly responded,
"It's a friend of the family".
She asked me to leave my number,
she would pass the message on.

He was at work and would be home by 5 p.m.
(I'm sitting there solo.)

I spent the afternoon cold and anxious,
whilst waiting by the phone.
17:15 p.m. passed, no call.
17:20 p.m. passed, no call.
At 17:30 p.m., the phone began to ring.
I started to panic—was it going to be him?
(I'm standing there solo.)

I answered the call and said, "Hello, who is calling"?
The voice said, "My name is Lloyd Irish".
I replied, "Do you have a daughter in England"?
He proudly replied, "Yes"!
(I'm standing there shivering.)

I asked, "Could you tell me her name, please"?
He quickly said, "Her name is
Remeaise Jennifer Irish".
(I stood there shaking.)

I splattered it out: "You are speaking to her".
His quick response was, in a Trinidadian accent,
"Girl, I've been searching for you
for more than three years".
I replied, "If you'd remembered
where we last lived, you could have knocked
on the landlord's door.
She could have told you we didn't live there anymore".

Well, he reminisced about the places
where he'd gone to look,
but unfortunately, they no longer existed.
"Never mind", he said, "you have found me.
I must make some calls so you can come and visit me".
(Still standing there solo.)

We spoke a little more; I had to clear my chest.
"Well, don't you worry, Dad, I didn't turn out too bad.
My mother's always been there. She really did her best".

Finding the Home

I do not want to live in a flat.
I'm definitely a snob to that.

Now, I don't believe in fairy tales,
that when I grow up, I'll get married,
have a house and kids and a car, blah, blah, blah.
Damn, I know, I have to work hard to get what I want.
What's the use of a house if there is no one to share it with you?
I was a twin and my twin brother died. I have always
said if I have children,
I don't want just one, but two children to keep each other company.

So, the hunting began, where would it be?
More to the fact, what could I afford comfortably?
I searched locally to be near my mum.
Sometimes it was too close for comfort.
I mean, a girl got to grow up some time.

I had four viewings to explore, in and around the area.
Hell no, I don't plan to live in a shoebox.
The prices were out of my reach.
So, I spoke to my uncle, the hierarchy,
and this is what he said to me.

"Young niece, you need to buy something decent,
so think further afar, you'd be better off,
and maybe be able to purchase a car".
So, I took his advice and searched near to him,
big value for money, the properties I viewed,
it could possibly be a house and not a flat.
I could never have imagined that.

The prospects looked good; the fourth place I viewed,
I was impressed and named my price to secure this home.
My agent was speaking on his mobile phone,
making an offer on my behalf.
I was so excited and began to laugh.

The suspense was too much; had I pushed my luck?
But he said, "They accepted your offer"!
I was elated. The agent stated, "You've sealed the deal"!
Now this moment was surreal.
Six weeks later, the keys were in my hand.
I bought my own home.

A two-bedroom mid-terrace house
they called it in the old days—a two-up, two-down.
That's what I bought, which consisted of a front lounge, dining room,
two bedrooms, a bathroom, and a garden too.

I was an independent woman;
I stripped wallpaper and sanded floors,
mixed the paint and applied it to the walls.
I even stained the doors in antique pine,
a mature colour of that time.

My hard work paid off,
and my goal of buying my own home
was achieved.

I didn't want to live my life as a spinster.
I loved my space but wanted to share it with someone.

Fleeing the Nest

It was time to flee the nest.
I'm thirty-five, you know.
I've saved for over two years,
so now it's time to go.
I've bought the basics that I need.
Thank God I don't have kids to feed.

I checked my mother's spice cupboard,
then made myself a list.
My goodness, so many spices,
I'll have to check the prices.

Four boxes now filled with tins of foods,
all from my favourite stores.
I started to have a panic attack
as I thought about doing my chores.

Well, now the day came,
and the van was filled.
It was time to say goodbye.

My mother stood on the step, trying to be brave.
I told her I would be back on every other day;
to help her with this challenge was the only way.

Well, I kept my promise.
Brought her food that I had cooked.
She really wasn't expecting this.
She gave me such a look.
She said, "Did you use a cookery book?
That was a shock for me".
She thought I would not cope.
I learned my skills from her.

I was taught by the best.
Now she had the time
to sit down and take a rest.

The proof was in her eating,
her favourite dish I cooked.
She scored me ten out of ten,
and I promised I'd do it again.

Each visit, I was expected
to come home with a dish.
This was now a test
on her wish list.

She never scored me again;
no need, said the big smile on her face.
Just to know I was happy and owning my own place.

A special day had come along—it was Mother's Day.
Mum came to my home for a special treat
and asked me, "What's on the menu today for us to eat"?
"Well"! I said, "one of your dishes of jerk pork and rice,
along with a glass of gin and tonic with ice".

She looked across the table.
When we sat down to eat,
she placed her palms together,
then we both said grace.
There was a little extra prayer:
"God bless my daughter's place".

The tears fell gracefully from her eyes,
she was choking up.
How proud she was to live to see
that I had finally grown up.

Ring My Bell

Mum was very fond of you.
She knew you were going to be faithful.
She treated you like her son,
as you were a genuine one.
She gave you the seven-inch record,
the title "You Can Ring My Bell"
that became our signature tune.
I can still remember it well.
The tune still lives on today.
It's aired on the radio,
it's also aired on TV.

My mum is in my thoughts
every time this song is played.
It also reminds me of the times
you came and rang my bell.
There were never any strings attached,
as we were just friends.
You were the one my mum trusted
to bring me back home nice and safe.
She didn't trust many people.

Our friendship lasted twenty years, on and off,
in-between, living our separate lives.
Somehow, we would reconnect.
Catch up on our journeys; then disappear again.
Mum was a woman who would scare
any young man pursuing her only daughter.
You certainly weren't intimidated by her.
You were never given the third-degree.
Maybe she knew she had to be gentle with you.
She loved and respected you. You were the son she always wished for.
You were respectful, caring, and thoughtful

about her wishes and gentle demands.
Your calm nature—an attribute she admired in you.
A perfect match in her mind.
You were a special kind.

I am sure that this relationship was a wish of hers.
She didn't frighten you away.
I knew there was a soft spot for you in her heart.
Well, her dream came true finally.
For her to see good friendships flourish
into a relationship between you and me.

It took us twenty years, but who's counting?
Fate is real; if people are meant to be together,
nothing is going to stop it from happening.
It's just a matter of time.

Where I am concerned,
you came into my life at the right time.
In fact, if I wasn't a shy girl, then maybe
we would have been together a lot sooner.
Sometimes, things happen;
or in my case, it didn't.

We were experiencing different lives;
for me, it was the freedom to grow
into the strong, independent woman
I've become over the years.
You were right to say
that you were waiting for me to grow up.

Well, now we've reunited;
you no longer need to ring my bell,
except if you've forgotten your keys.
You can ring the bell to my heart.

Is It Coincidental?

There have been many occasions
when we have crossed paths.
Was this a little sign?
It's taken twenty years, you know.

You were meant to be mine.
Being so naïve, I did not see the signs.
Before I met you, I knew your family.
You were in the same neighbourhood,
around the corner from me.

When at my university one day,
who should I see?
My neighbour, three houses
down the road from me,
who turned out to be a member
of your family.

He invited me to hang out
at the local church,
where his cousins were all present,
as they had formed a little band.
You were their bass guitar player,
with fine fingers plucking strings,
sweet music to my ears.
You were already spoken for.
I had to respect that fact.

I was not a forward girl.
I was far too shy
to express my feelings
about the way I felt.
You were the perfect gentleman.

Every time we all went out,
you'd always walk me to my door
to make sure I was safe.

A little kiss on the face.
And a little wave goodbye.

My mother grew so fond of you
but was so very strict.
She always called you "son",
as if one day she knew
we would meet on different grounds,
and then we'd become two.
It was her wish for you to marry me,
and she would feel contented if it came true.

You were the son she always wanted:
kind, loving, and true.
The perfect son-in-law was granted
twenty years later; it was surely meant to be.
As now it's over forty years that you have known me.

We now have two children, a small second family.
For you were once married and had three lovely boys
who have grown into fine young men.

I am proud my children know their older brothers,
a bond that can't be broken.
Through a social network, they connected,
without my knowledge.

I was happy they could keep in touch
and have fine role models
they could call upon whenever they needed guidance.

Reunited and Found Love

It's never too late.
Now I need to find me a date.
My friends would phone me,
ask if I fancied going out.

Virtually every weekend,
I would rave to the max.
I never found that special one.

My friends were on that mission too.
We met all sorts—the young and the old.
I was stuck in-between.

Thirty-five and still looking for the one person
who would bring happiness
and laughter to my crib.

They say all good things
come to those who wait.
How long is it going to take?

My life has really begun now.
I am free to explore and be me.
Am I being impatient, or am I just following my dreams?

I've thought about how I'd like to live my life
but have high expectations.
The first was to buy my own home.
Not following the trend of having a child,
to get a flat from the council.

That was the jump-start for some.
Not my way to start out in life.

My preference was to be in a relationship
with the right person for me:
Mr. Compatible.

I am a creative, so if we have this in common,
it would be a good start; also, a sense of humour.
I am a bubbly person, so happiness is a must.

I've always wished for these things.
The priorities for my life are to have someone
who could do the things I was unable to do.

I am an independent woman.
I will not settle for just any man who comes along.
He has to be the one who will be there for the long haul.
I'm on a journey of becoming me.

I need someone who admires that part of my life.
Someone who wants me to share his world and he mine.
Or what is the point?
I've come this far by myself.

One fine Saturday afternoon,
I popped into my local market.
I was now into the neo-soul genre of music.
I was dressed in my wide-legged trousers and a halter top,
and my hair was covered in an African wrap.
I loved Erykah Badu's style of dressing;
this was my influence at the time.
I decided to buy her CD.

I had reunited with my very first secret love.
Well, not himself, but his two younger brothers.
We hugged and chatted a little.
The eldest of the two handed his mobile phone to me.

This was the beginning of the reunion.

The friendship rekindled as grown adults.
We found out we had a lot in common.
We took our time and reminisced of the old days.

I confessed that I had feelings,
but I was too shy to express them to him.
It was never the right time. Twenty years later.
No point holding back, the feelings were mutual.

My mother had already known from way back
that we were the perfect match.
Education and a foundation were the priorities instilled in me.

My hang-up was the age difference between us;
you were twenty-three months younger than me.
Looking back, what a waste of those years.
As I said, it's never too late.

Sometimes, it's in God's plan.
We need to grow as individuals. To first love ourselves
before loving and growing together.

I Didn't Know It Yet

I found my soul mate, although neither of us knew it yet.
He was literally on my doorstep.
If someone predicted this would have happened,
I'm sure I would have placed a £10 bet.

Imagine, all this time growing up in the same neighbourhood.
I used to play games on my street with his cousins.
We still hadn't crossed paths yet.

I was not allowed to turn the street corner on the end of my road.
My mother said she wanted to be able to see me and know that I was safe.
I spent seven years growing up in the same neighbourhood,
running errands for my mother down to the corner shop;
then venturing farther to the local markets,
Hammersmith and Shepherds Bush.

I used to have to take my mother's shopping trolley
to manage all the shopping she needed.
Shepherds Bush for the Caribbean vegetables,
plantains, yams, coco, sweet potatoes and fruits such as
Julie mangoes, Jamaican oranges,
ugli fruit, sorrel, and bunches of guinep,
also known by the name of skinup in Grenada.

Hammersmith market, which was on my doorstep,
was the second market I would've visited.
Every Saturday morning, it was my job
to buy the carrots, cabbages, beetroots,
and a pint of prawns along with some coley fish.

My friends used to take the mickey out of me
if they happened to bump into me doing the shopping.
I knew I was developing my life skills

and also helping my mother.

The years went by, and it was time for college.
That was when I met my soul mate, although I still didn't know it.
I was introduced to him by his cousin, who came to my college
when I had started my second year of study.

I was invited to the local church hall one day by his cousin Lloyd
to listen to the band they had formed.
Listening to Kenny play the bass guitar was music to my ears.
I enjoyed listening to reggae and soul music at that time.
I made new friends and met other members of the family.

This was during the late seventies.
A friendship was built over time.
We would cross paths over the years; in fact, just three times.
I remember each time well as if it were yesterday.

The third time we crossed paths, it was now the 1990s.

I bumped into your younger brothers.
The eldest of the two, he was on his mobile after we exchanged hugs.
Then he passed his mobile to me.

I remember hearing your words: "Which Jennifer"?
I heard your voice and asked, "How many Jennifers do you know"?
The name you knew me by, growing up in the same area,
my local friends called me by my middle name,
as that's what my mother called me
in the home and in the neighbourhood.

You were at the end of another relationship.
I felt sad that things did not end happily ever after.
This was a time when I was now mature
and had my independence.

I decided to rekindle our friendship
that had never been lost but just put on hold
whilst we were getting on with our own lives.
I remember we spoke about everything.
I plucked up the courage to let you know
how I felt from the very first time I set eyes on you.
You were acknowledging the same feelings.

I obviously did not know that all these years I was even your type.
I felt it was now or never, as I was not getting any younger.
Well, I was laying my cards on the table.
You were shocked by how I'd grown up as a woman.

I was in the middle of a commission, sewing a wedding dress,
a maid of honour dress, and a flower girl dress for the bride's daughter.
I invited you to attend the wedding with me
and realised the friendship
had remained the same, with no strings attached.
But we had now grown into adults who had lived our lives.

It was like old times; Mum was so glad to see you again
but a bit suspicious this time,
as she wasn't sure what was going on.
Why you sprung up after all these years.
With a little patience, she was convinced you were still
an honourable young man.

When you were free, we started a relationship.
I can't say I wasn't nervous, as you were a good friend,
one I could confide in about anything.
I prayed it did not spoil the friendship we had.

We had a lot in common; I realised that after a while.
We both loved going to car boots; we were both artists.
A shared love of making things.

What I was unable to do, you were able to do.
We certainly complemented each other's skills.

I remember our first Valentine's Day.
You searched everywhere for my favourite flowers.
Also, the little gift you gave me: the cups.
A couple linking their arms together.
The message on their bums said, "We fit together".

I remember searching for the perfect card
that expressed the way I felt about you.
That was something I would carefully choose
for someone as special as you.

The relationship blossomed.
We certainly had our highs and a few lows.
But through communication,
we worked things out together.

Why Are Relationships So Complicated?

Why can't people fall in love at first sight?
Is it such a crime? Who are we hurting?
Love can happen the first time
you set eyes on someone.
It doesn't mean you'll tell each other.
Your feelings are your feelings.

I know because it happened to me.
Two people can become one.
What is love? Learning to give and take,
openness to each other's thoughts and feelings,
valuing each other's strengths,
helping them with their weaknesses,
and enjoying each other's company.

Well, for me, it is growing together.
Taking each day a step at a time;
finding ways to make each of us happy.
Being loved and cared for
and giving the same back.
It takes two in the first place.

So we work together and complement
each other's abilities.
So this is my take on my relationship.

The Eco-Fashion Show

Being mentored to make this happen,
I really didn't have time for too much yapping.
I think about all I'm expected to do.
I really should have just hired you too.

First, recruiting the students to make this all happen.
Then finding a place to demonstrate
all the skills that were needed to carry out the tasks
for all the students who would be attending my class.

Weeks of planning, I was under so much stress.
Looking at the piles of clothes creating such a mess.
Eventually, when sorted, they'd become a dress.

Students achieve the goals of sewing and cutting,
designing their ideas by sketching on paper.
Patterns are cut and fabrics cut later.

Garments are ready for models to fit.
The children are asked to find a chair to sit.
Tene is wearing the main statement piece;
her crown adorns her head.
The waves of chiffon gently cascading down her back
with a shimmery sparkle showing the ocean's blue
that are filled with the plastic problems that cling to her.
Adults turn up, as they've been chosen to model.
The music is played for them to go waddle.

Everybody's ready for the big day.
So many people with important roles to play:
the makeup artist, hairdresser, and photographer too.
Everyone knows exactly what to do.

The children are getting ready to take to the stage.
We file them in one by one according to their age.
In comes the youngest child as cute as can be,
wearing a T-shirt that says Save Energy.
In comes the next child as bold as can be.
His top says Recycled by Me!

The others walk in a single file until the catwalk is full.
A younger child complains; he does not want to be pulled.
As all the children are now on stage,
in comes the star of the show.

Tene walking with two children by her side;
they carry a denim whale, which was washed up from the ocean.
They bend their young heads, as if they're ashamed.
Tene stands tall and elegant, the queen of the sea.
She turns and leaves us with this image in our minds.

Then in comes Shania wearing her favourite wedge.
She sings for the final part of the show.
I see the stage manager turn her programme page.
The children see her signal to depart from the stage.

There was so much pressure
to meet the goals ahead.
Teaching, marketing, and modelling sessions too.
So much goes into making a show, so much work to do.
I really thought the people would understand;
the scale of tasks I had to do was totally in my hands.

Where did the time go?
I really didn't know
how doing something I loved
could make me feel so low.

We the people created the plastic problem.
Instead of saving trees, we have polluted the air
and polluted the seas.
We need to do something to save mankind.
We created the problem and now we need to fix it.

When You Look in the Mirror

When you look in the mirror, who do you see?
Do you see a reflection of you?
Lift up your head, lift it up high.
You can hold your own and reach for the sky.

You have pure melanin, you have been blessed.
You are special, just like the rest.
Don't underestimate yourself
or your capabilities.

You are strong and black.
You've carried heavier loads on your back.

Look forward and look beyond.
Onwards and upwards.
Keep singing your songs.

Hard work always pays off.
Believe what I say.
There is never a shorter way.

Live by good morals and pass on those skills,
for each one teaches one as we climb up those hills.
You will be rewarded by sticking to the plan.
Rome wasn't built in a day.
You will turn out to be a fine young man.

Look at the bigger picture
and what we could achieve
by following the right path
for a better future.

One-off Wonder Is My Name

One-off Wonder is my name,
there is never going to be another.
I am unique—I came from inside my mother.
She only ever had one lover.

One-off Wonder is my name,
I was not born in vain.
There is a reason for this title.
Life is certainly no game.

One-off Wonder is my name,
I will never feel ashamed.
I was given a precious life.
I will continue to live and strive.

Like-minded People

Frustrated with not hearing about places to go.
Not having the technology we have now, such as Facebook,
Twitter, and Instagram.
I heard people reciting black poetry at my workplace,
also from friends who sing.
I thought about taking action; word of mouth spread here and there.
I thought about venues, but why waste money?
I held the event in my home.
So much talent was around me sharing their voices
about their own choices on subjects that concerned us all.
One poem was read out by a friend of mine.
It was called: Was it right to be a mother at forty?
Who are we to judge God's gift? It's always a blessing.
We celebrated each other's gifts from God.
No judgment but questions; what inspired each other's poem or song?
The evening came to an end; it never took place in my home again.
People networked and got back to their lives.
Writing for their own reasons; healing, singing, bleeding their words.
I brought people together to share what they loved
and what I truly loved.
Now I see where my passion has grown.
Now I've started writing poetry of my own.

Part Three

POEMS ABOUT ISSUES
THAT CONCERN ME

Be Happy in Your Skin

Ladies, be proud of your melanin.
Be proud of the skin you're in.
Be grateful for what you have been given.
After all, you are still living.

No need for making changes.
God blessed you individually
so you could be unique.
Why would you crave something
that's not in your own genetics?

On the flip side, look at what is happening.
Women are spending fortunes
to change the way they look.
They want blond hair, Brazilian weaves,
pumped lips, facelifts, big hips,
big boobs, tight vagina, and bling, bling on your ting.

Now they bleach their skin.
Thank God for your blessings.
Give thanks for what you have.
Live your best life—embrace and enjoy it,
for tomorrow is not promised.

When you see a sister and she looks good,
give her the praise she so deserves.

Make her day in this small way.
It doesn't cost a thing.

What Is Wrong with Some People?

What is wrong with some people?
Why do they hate us so much?
Haven't our ancestors gone through enough?
Come on! We were here first—accept that fact.
You stole us from our motherlands
to places far and beyond.
You forced us to work your lands for free.
No money to feed our own family.
Why were you born? Why were we born?
Was it not for the same reasons?
God made people of all colours
so there would be a variety.
We are all humans.
We have the same blood
that's pumping from our hearts
and flowing through our bodies;
that's what keeps us alive.
So what makes you think we are the inferior ones
to be used and abused for your wealth and happiness?
We were all born from man and woman.

Many years of abuse and name-calling:
ugly, nappy head, nigger, big lips, big hips.
Some of us took these words to heart;
as a result, we have suffered
from low self-esteem.
We have changed the way we look,
just trying to be accepted.
We have bleached our skin to look lighter;
we have weaved our hair to look European;
and a few other things added to the list.
Isn't it funny, we have now woken up and seen the light?

The ones who have profited off our free labour
actually condemned us and hated us
for the beauty we carried around.

We witness today the wheels have turned;
the privileged ones have always been jealous
of the colour of our skin.
The beautiful melanin.
The coils we are wearing.

They go on holiday to colour their skin.
Don't want to be in the shoes we're wearing.
They braid their hair—that was our thing
from the very beginning.
They inject their lips to get puffed lips.
They inject their hips and their tits.
Do you see where I'm going with this?
Wake up! Some of you people,
please don't hate us.

We showed you our beauty.
You knocked us down.
We are rising up and wearing our crowns.
Please do not go around wearing a frown.

What Has Happened to Our Young People?

What have we done to our young people?
Why are they killing so much?
Why are they killing each other:
their brother, a baby, your mother, your father?

Why do they feel they need to get everything so quickly?
Admittedly, society has changed through having all this
technology.
We want quick-speed internet services;
the young want fast earnings.
Pressure from social media on how people
have made their first millions.

Getting bombarded with people
who reckon they know how you can get rich quick.
I mean, who doesn't want to know how to
make money faster
so they can buy cars, houses,
and everything under the sun?

So now we have come to this.
Over the years, more and more young ones
are getting into postcode wars.
Imagine you can't enter your own neighbourhood,
or anyone else's, as this is now a problem.
Now young people are scared; their lives being threatened.
So the result is, carrying guns and knives for protection?
Was I naive to think years ago
it only happened abroad?

Well, now it's here, and it's so out of control.
This is not cool or how they should roll.

Where is the love for your brothers and sisters?
Every day on the news, we see
families grieving for the loss of a child.
There are knifings and shootings
happening far too much
in the UK, somewhere.
We are totally in despair.

Mothers and fathers, these are children of God.
Why have they turned into monsters?
When is it going to stop?

I grieve for sons and daughters I don't even know;
but I know it's a loss in our black community.
We are all responsible for the next generation.
This problem needs to be addressed.
How do we raise these kids
and keep them off the streets?
Teach them how to love one another,
their sisters, and brothers.

Please look out and do what you can
to help them grow into decent young men and women.
Right now, they're still young children,
dying all over the streets,
there's no one looking out for them.
For fear of getting caught up in the conflicts,
we have failed our young people.
We have stripped them from their youth.
Saving money for wars
by shutting down the youth clubs
and depriving them of what they used to have,
which was a safe environment to play
in communities that were manned.

What Has Happened to the Family?

Tell me, what has happened to our family?
Why are we all so me, me, me?
I am the same as I'll always be,
trying to support all my family.
Why is it when we need help,
nobody uses their initiative
or volunteers to help out?

When a loved one is suffering,
we all seem not to have the time.
Please remember, this is our family line.
We assume it's someone else's problem;
we have our own jobs to do
to carry out the responsibility.
It really comes down to you.

We are all grown up and have children.
We need to consider we're not alone.
We all have a life to live
with priorities in our hands.

So when things happen to the family,
it is our duty to all chip in.

Please remember the load we bare
can wear one person down thin.
I love all of my family;
we all have minds of our own.
But please check in from time to time,
and not just over the phone.
We can't see what's really happening
by speaking over the phone.

So please go check on your family
by visiting them in their home.
Life is way too short,
for oh, I should have done more!
When you had your health and strength,
there's so much that could have been done.
But do not leave the responsibility to just only one.

We all have to answer to the good Lord
when he asks, "What have we done to help others"?
Hope you said you also helped a friend.

To All the Childless Mothers

You may not have been blessed with children;
it may not have been God's plan.
It doesn't mean you don't care for others in your life
just like a mother would.
You might have cared for a sibling.
My mother was cared for by her older sister,
who was herself unable to conceive children.

My mother had seven siblings in her family,
her parents had a food business, so every
hand was on deck to help them.
Neighbours' children would be there at the
end of the day to get their dinner.
The Caribbean families back in the day
shared the care amongst family members;
be it a grandmother, auntie, or older siblings,
this was the normal thing in our culture.

My godmother stepped up for her babysitting duties;
we had a very close bond until she passed away.
She was defeated by the battle of cancer.
In the Caribbean, everyone in the community was in charge
of raising the children and had permission
to tell a child off for misbehaving.

Children respected their elders;
if they didn't, their parents would soon hear about it.
In life, we take care of our parents
when they can't take care of themselves.
The roles reverse, and you are the responsible one for their well-being.

My point is you are valued as if you were everyone's mother and
deserve to be acknowledged on Mother's Day, just like the rest of us.
My wish today is that if you know someone who fits the roles
I have mentioned, take them some flowers or buy them some chocolates
to show you care.

Just to show your appreciation.
If I knew any of these people, I would honour their good work.
You may not be able to make them breakfast in bed,
but a card on Mother's Day is just as good a gesture.

Part Four

CARING THOUGHTS

Compassion

Compassion is everything right now.
We are living in a sad world of destruction.
So many people are dying all over the world for numerous reasons.
I know we cannot live forever,
but some are taken too soon, and I ask the question why?
I know I am not the only one to have lost a loved one;
in fact, I have lost several loved ones—not all are related.
The first loss I can remember was my grandmother,
whom I have never met but have written to her since the age of seven.
She died aged seventy-two from a stroke.
My mother wasn't able to travel to Jamaica
for her own mother's funeral due to health issues.
The second person I lost was my Aunt Mina, who named me
Remeaise.
I have photos of her but never got to know her.
She died of the dreaded C—yes, cancer.
This was when I was eleven years of age.
This was tragic for her. To add to this,
two other uncles died in the same month.
Yes, you guessed it: cancer.
So in one month, three of her siblings died.
My mother, due to health reasons, could not travel.
So compassion—is it enough to say I have a lot of compassion for people
and their losses? Yes, I certainly do.
I've watched the family break down in so many ways.
I've watched others suffer through the loss of someone close to them.
The biggest hurt was watching my own mother
going through mental health problems daily.
I remember I was just over five years old.
My school picked up that something wasn't quite right.
My mother took pride in keeping me clean and tidy for school;
but one morning, looking at how I came to school raised alarm bells.

The way I was dressed and my hair so
untidy, they knew this was not normal.
That caused concern in their eyes and thankfully
gave my mother and myself some support needed.
I'll be ever grateful for that,
or I might not have been here to tell the story.
I've lost my two godmothers: Ruby and Ina.
Then my Auntie Doris at eighty-one years of age.
Imagine, she came to the United Kingdom at the age of eighty.
She didn't last very long with our weather and her health.
She had all her faculties; she didn't even wear glasses.
She could read with no difficulty.
The only problem she had was that she was a diabetic.
She had a small leg injury whilst in the UK, then suffered an infection.
This caused her to have her toes—and then finally a leg—amputated
before she died.
Then my favourite uncle/father Bifore died at the age of ninety-six.
He had buried all his siblings and parents so far,
except one brother called Eric,
who is still alive today, aged ninety.
I have been there too many times grieving
and now had to put my cat down
due to serious health issues.
It was better for her to be put out of her pain.
I know she was loved and spoilt by us all;
she was a loyal and cheeky cat for ten years.
She took her time to come out of her shell.
All lives matter to me.

Thank You, Mum

Thank you for bringing me into this world,
for teaching me all the things I needed to know to survive.
I have always looked up to you
but did not always agree with your way of raising me.
Looking back now,
I fully understand why you were making those decisions:
you simply loved me.
Old schooling was old schooling,
and it was the only way you knew how to bring me up.
You had your role models and your skills passed down from your parents.
My life could have taken a different path,
but you tried to protect me from the vultures out there.
I remember you used to say, "Them damn vultures are out there".
This was said every time I wanted to go out with my friends.
I used to convince you that I would be fine and could look after myself.
I wanted to learn from my own mistakes.
Becoming a mother at a later age, I was filled with
knowledge, wisdom, and understanding
that you instilled in me. I knew your reasons were valid;
after all, I was the only survivor of your three children.
Sadly, your firstborn, Aloysius, died at the age of six months in Jamaica.

Then I was part of a twin, but my brother was too weak and died.
I survived and obviously was a little fighter for life.
In memory of this, I registered my son,
Aloysius, as his middle name
so my brother would never be forgotten.
When I had my daughter, she was registered with your name.
Alma is her middle name so you would never be forgotten.
Thank the good Lord for letting you live
to see two beautiful grandchildren,
making you proud of the next generation.

I tell them stories all the time
to keep our memories alive.
I used you as a reference if I had issues with their behaviour.
I would tell them Grandma would do things differently.
Certain things that were done in the 1960s
were soon abolished by the government.
So people could get arrested or children were taken away,
for child protection times have changed.
Rights are taken away from parents
for the way they discipline their children.
Smacking is not allowed—it didn't kill me.
I am a better person for it.
I have had to find different ways of disciplining my children.
There would be more verbal reasoning.
Your grandchildren are proud to have known you;
for a short time, you were in their lives.

God knew it was time for you to carry on your good work
with him in the great heavens above.
I love you unconditionally.
You're always in my heart and in my daily ups and downs.
From:
Your same loving daughter.

To All of the Readers

To all of my interested readers,
who have supported me,
this is dedicated to you.
Through this, my writing journey.

Everything I've written here
is from my point of view.
This has been true to my thoughts and words,
but this is just the beginning.
I am creating more—I'm promising.

The poems are written to urge people of all ages
to never give up on their dreams.
We all go through some struggles;
that's normality in real life.

If we didn't go through struggles,
then we would not appreciate life.

Life would be so boring
if we were all the same.
We only have one life to live.
And this one's not a game.

Let's get on and live it
to the best we possibly can.
Working to help each other grow as one.

Acknowledgments

There are a few people who have helped me to complete my book, and without their help, it would have been a struggle.

First, to my mother, Mehala Dawson, for always encouraging me to do my best and to work hard for everything I want to achieve in life.

To my family, especially my hubby, who put up with the clicking noise of my typing and the light on whilst he tried to sleep.

I'd like to thank Jorell Cave for making my front cover vision come to life.

I want to express my gratitude to my dear friend Deborah Cook for patiently reading and drawing illustrations for a selection of short poems in my book.

My thanks goes out to Nuno for listening to my specific needs in formatting my interior and exterior of my book.

Finally, a big thanks to Shayla Raquel for copyediting my book and keeping the tone of my voice throughout and helping me to make it the best it could be.

About the Author

Remeaise Irish-Downes is a survivor of many incidents, for which she is truly grateful to God. She prays daily and offers thanks to God for the blessings he brings her. She is married to a wonderful man named Kenny and is a mother to two young adults, Chauntier and Shania. She is a creative, energetic, and skillful woman who enjoys travelling and meeting different people from around the globe. She enjoys dancing, cooking, and eating colourful food.

Remeaise grows her own fruit and vegetables and has been told that she has green fingers. She is always creating things that are sewn, knitted, or crocheted—or even glued together, as she helps her son to make carnival costumes. Remeaise is the author of A Collection of Poems by Black British Poet.

Connect with the Author
Facebook.com/remeaiseoneoffwonder
Instagram.com/remeaiseoneoffwonder
www.remeaise.com